Spelling

Ages 5–7

quick quizzes

jam

coat

he

strong

Jill Atkins

er, ir and ur

Write er, ir or ur in each gap to make a word.

1 g___l

2 v___b

3 c___l

4 ch___ch

5 h___b

6 b___d

7 st___

8 b___st

9 d___t

10 h___

11 f___st

12 Th___sday

13 h___t

14 t___m

15 p___son

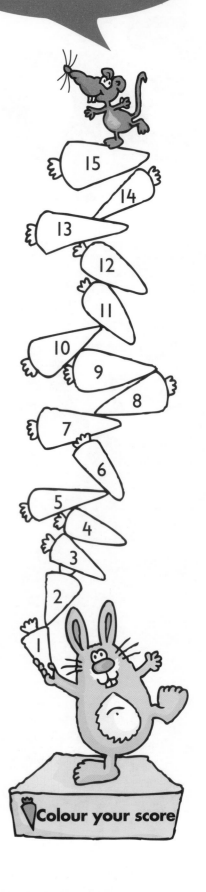

Remember, er, ir and ur have the same sound.

15
14
13
12
11
10
9
8
7
6
5
4
3
2
1

Colour your score

2

Plurals: -s or -es

Add **s** or **es** to make each noun plural.

1 banana____

2 hedge____

3 book____

4 witch____

5 duck____

6 buzz____

7 kite____

8 match____

9 dish____

10 frog____

11 leg____

12 bus____

13 bank____

14 hutch____

15 cow____

Nouns ending in **zz, s, sh** and **tch** need **es** to make them plural.

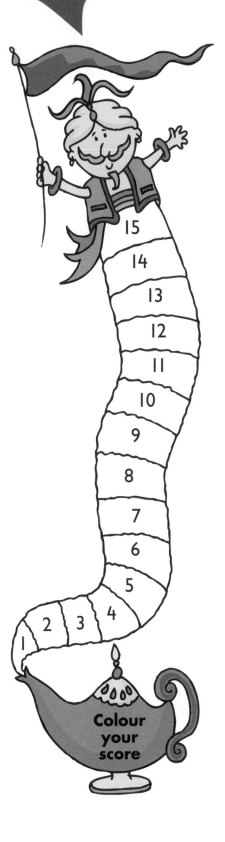

15
14
13
12
11
10
9
8
7
6
5
4
3
2
1

Colour your score

3

Word endings: -tch or -ch

Use tch or ch to end each word.

1 hu_____

2 fe_____

3 mu_____

4 ca_____

5 rea_____

6 di_____

7 pin_____

8 pa_____

9 ri_____

10 ar_____

11 tha_____

12 su_____

13 ma_____

14 bea_____

15 i_____

> tch and ch have the same sound.

15
14
13
12
11
10
9
8
7
6
5
4
3
2
1

Colour your score

4

Wh- question words

Write **What**, **When**, **Where**, **Why** or **Which** at the start of each sentence.

These are words that often go at the beginning of questions.

1 _____ is your favourite animal?

2 _____ are you laughing?

3 _____ does your friend come from?

4 _____ can you come to my house to play?

5 _____ is the best time for your party?

6 _____ are there so many stars in the sky?

7 _____ train will you catch?

8 _____ time do you go to bed?

9 _____ girl scored the winning goal?

10 _____ will you know who has won?

11 _____ would you like for your birthday?

12 _____ apple would you like?

12
11
10
9
8
7
6
5
4
3
2
1

Colour your score

5

-ing and -ed

Add ing and ed to each verb to make new forms of the verb.

You don't need to change the spellings of these verbs first.

1 farm _____ _____

2 storm _____ _____

3 hatch _____ _____

4 kick _____ _____

5 bang _____ _____

6 thank _____ _____

7 hiss _____ _____

8 call _____ _____

9 buzz _____ _____

10 puff _____ _____

11 milk _____ _____

12 jump _____ _____

13 shock _____ _____

14 growl _____ _____

15 bark _____ _____

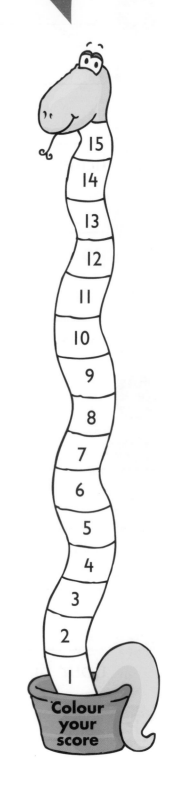

15
14
13
12
11
10
9
8
7
6
5
4
3
2
1
Colour your score

More –ing and –ed

Add **ing** and **ed** to each verb.

1 hum _____ _____

2 smile _____ _____

3 knit _____ _____

4 hop _____ _____

5 shave _____ _____

6 clap _____ _____

7 shade _____ _____

8 skate _____ _____

9 chat _____ _____

10 slice _____ _____

11 skip _____ _____

12 shape _____ _____

13 rob _____ _____

14 plan _____ _____

15 grin _____ _____

Change the spellings before you add **ing** or **ed** to the end.

Colour your score

7

Prefixes: un–

Write the prefix **un** before each of these words.

un often makes a word with the opposite meaning.

1 ___block

2 ___equal

3 ___hook

4 ___happy

5 ___pack

6 ___even

7 ___able

8 ___cover

9 ___clear

10 ___afraid

11 ___kind

12 ___helpful

13 ___plug

14 ___ripe

15 ___well

Colour your score

15
14
13
12
11
10
9
8
7
6
5
4
3
2
1

-ve words

Choose a word that ends with ve to complete each sentence.

love	drive	arrive	hive	gave
above	live	five	brave	cave

1. Bees make honey in a _____.

2. My friends began to _____ at my party.

3. Dad said that I was very _____ when I hurt my leg.

4. The three little pigs _____ in three little houses.

5. Grandad _____ me a fantastic train set.

6. In winter, the bear hibernated deep inside a dark _____.

7. A helicopter hovered _____ us this morning.

8. I _____ my little pet rabbit, Rosy, very much.

9. I have _____ toes on each foot.

10. We had to _____ for a long time before we reached the sea.

Colour your score

9

-er and -est

Add **er** and **est** to each adjective to make new words.

You may need to double the consonant or drop the **e** at the end of the word first.

1 long _____ _____

2 short _____ _____

3 tall _____ _____

4 thick _____ _____

5 soft _____ _____

6 bright _____ _____

7 dark _____ _____

8 mad _____ _____

9 red _____ _____

10 large _____ _____

11 simple _____ _____

12 nice _____ _____

13 thin _____ _____

14 big _____ _____

15 gentle _____ _____

Colour your score

Apostrophes

Add an **apostrophe** and s to these singular nouns.

1 the dog____ bone

2 the man____ hat

3 the girl____ hair

4 the boy____ socks

5 the cat____ whiskers

6 the lady____ shoes

7 the car____ horn

8 the elephant____ trunk

9 the train____ whistle

10 the pig____ curly tail

11 the bird____ wing

12 the cow____ calf

13 the windmill____ sails

14 the horse____ saddle

15 the mouse____ nest

Use an apostrophe when something belongs to something or someone.

Colour your score

Changing y to i

Add er and est to these adjectives.

1 silly _____ _____

2 angry _____ _____

3 happy _____ _____

4 heavy _____ _____

Add es and ed to these verbs.

5 cry _____ _____

6 marry _____ _____

7 hurry _____ _____

8 fry _____ _____

Make these nouns plural.

9 baby _____

10 family _____

11 lorry _____

12 lady _____

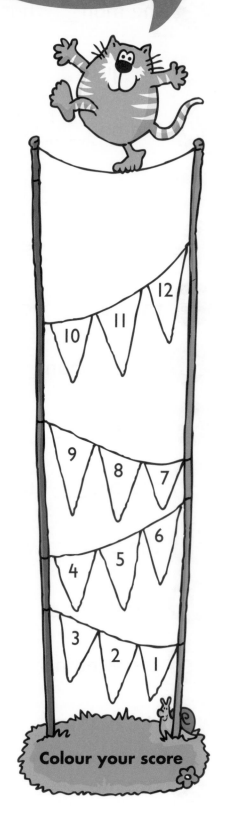

You need to change y to i first.

Colour your score

12

Suffixes: –ment or –ness

Circle the word with the correct suffix in each sentence.

A suffix goes at the end of a word.

1. The children crept out into the **darkness** / **darkment**.

2. The bus driver asked for **payness** / **payment** for our tickets.

3. The boy felt very weak after his **illness** / **illment**.

4. We stared in **amazeness** / **amazement** at the shooting stars.

5. The family enjoyed the **entertainness** / **entertainment** at the holiday club.

6. I was shocked at the girl's **rudeness** / **rudement** to her mum.

7. My sunglasses protect my eyes from the **brightness** / **brightment** of the sun.

8. The lady thanked me for my **kindness** / **kindment** when I helped her.

9. My tummy fluttered with **exciteness** / **excitement** as we set off.

10. The boy was given a **punishness** / **punishment** for breaking the window.

11. I was full of **sadness** / **sadment** when my gran went home.

12. It gives my dad **enjoyness** / **enjoyment** to watch me play football.

12
11
10
9
8
7
6
5
4
3
2
1

Colour your score

Syllables

How many **syllables** are there in each animal word?

Draw lines between the syllables, then count the syllables.

1 z e b r a ☐

2 e l e p h a n t ☐

3 k a n g a r o o ☐

4 c h i m p a n z e e ☐

5 h i p p o p o t a m u s ☐

6 c a t e r p i l l a r ☐

7 b u t t e r f l y ☐

8 t i g e r ☐

9 a n t e l o p e ☐

10 b a b o o n ☐

11 b u f f a l o ☐

12 c o c k a t o o ☐

13 a l l i g a t o r ☐

14 t a r a n t u l a ☐

15 r a t t l e s n a k e ☐

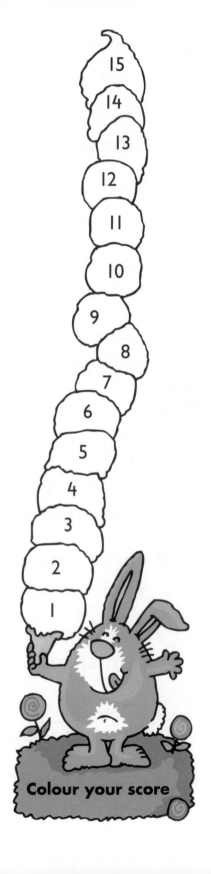

15
14
13
12
11
10
9
8
7
6
5
4
3
2
1

Colour your score

Homophones

Write **there**, **their** or **they're** in each sentence.

1 The children put on _____ hats and coats.

2 _____ is going to be snow tomorrow.

3 I saw a fox over _____ in the trees.

4 _____ working very hard to finish on time.

5 I think _____ going swimming today.

6 The birds built _____ nest in the apple tree.

Write **here** or **hear** in each sentence.

7 Can you _____ that aeroplane flying over?

8 Come over _____ and sit down for story time.

9 _____ is my favourite teddy.

10 I didn't _____ you when you called.

11 I love to _____ the birds singing in the garden.

12 I came _____ to buy some new shoes.

12
11
10
9
8
7
6
5
4
3
2
1

Colour your score

a_e, ay or ai words

Underline the **correct** spelling of each word.

1 We went sailing on the **lake / layk / laik**.

2 The hen sat on her nest and **lade / layd / laid** an egg.

3 There are only ten **dase / days / dais** until my party.

4 You are going as slowly as a **snale / snayl / snail**.

5 The robin flew **awae / away / awai** when I went near.

6 My grandad helped me **bake / bayk / baik** some biscuits.

7 I put some **hae / hay / hai** in the rabbit's hutch.

8 I am going to **pante / paynt / paint** a picture of my family.

9 The girl showed how she could **skate / skayt / skait** very fast on the ice.

10 My mum wears a silver **chane / chayn / chain** round her neck.

11 I am going to **stae / stay / stai** with my cousins in the summer.

12 The **snake / snayk / snaik** slithered along the dusty ground.

a_e, ay and ai sound the same, so see if you know the correct ones.

Colour your score

16

When dge or ge say 'j'

Tick the correct spelling of each word.
Use the pictures to help you.

dge and ge usually make a soft j sound.

1 cadge ☐ cage ☐

2 orange ☐ orandge ☐

3 andgel ☐ angel ☐

4 sausadge ☐ sausage ☐

5 slege ☐ sledge ☐

6 bridge ☐ brige ☐

7 bandadge ☐ bandage ☐

8 cabbage ☐ cabbadge ☐

9 bage ☐ badge ☐

10 cottadge ☐ cottage ☐

11 fridge ☐ frige ☐

12 badger ☐ bager ☐

Colour your score

More homophones

Write the correct word in each sentence.

Check the meaning of each word if you need to.

one or **won?**

1 At the party, I _____ a prize for best disco dancing.

2 Mum said I could have only _____ cake.

3 _____ day, a little old woman baked a gingerbread man.

4 On sports day, I raced as fast as I could and _____.

to, **too** or **two?**

5 I saw a huge dog on my way _____ school.

6 If you go to the fair, can I come _____?

7 I've got one sister and _____ brothers.

8 I felt ill after eating _____ much ice cream.

where or **wear?**

9 I needed to _____ my coat because it was cold.

10 I could not remember _____ I had put my book.

11 You can't play with my toys because you might _____ them out.

12 _____ are you going?

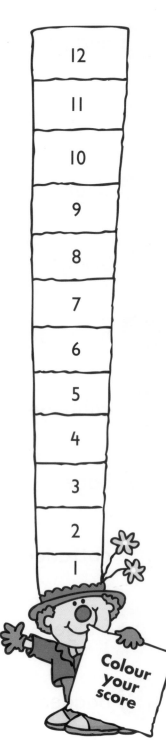

12
11
10
9
8
7
6
5
4
3
2
1

Colour your score

Contractions

Write the **contraction** for each set of words.

1 I am _____

2 we will _____

3 do not _____

4 cannot _____

5 it is _____

6 I will _____

7 here is _____

Turn each **contraction** back into the words it came from.

8 didn't _____

9 she's _____

10 they're _____

11 hasn't _____

12 aren't _____

13 I've _____

14 couldn't _____

14
13
12
11
10
9
8
7
6
5
4
3
2
1

Colour your score

19

Finding rhymes

Write a word that **rhymes** with the word in blue.

Remember to use the same spelling at the end of your word.

1 find   k_____

2 door   p_____

3 fast   l_____

4 come   s_____

5 class   gr_____

6 could   w_____

7 child   w_____

8 cold   g_____

9 break   st_____

10 path   b_____

11 prove   m_____

12 any   m_____

13 ask   t_____

14 pull   f_____

15 ghost   m_____

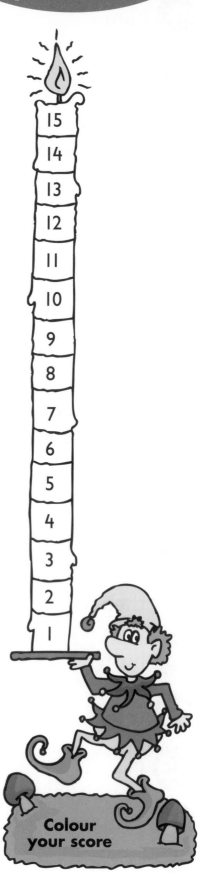

Colour your score

20

Suffixes: –ful or –less

Write **ful** or **less** at the end of
each word.

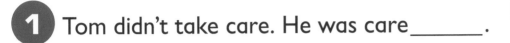

When **ful** is
a suffix, it has
only one l.

1 Tom didn't take care. He was care_____.

2 Mia fell and hurt her arm. It was pain_____.

3 The painting had many bright colours.
It was colour_____.

4 The phone has no cord. It is cord_____.

5 There were no clouds in the sky. The sky
was cloud_____.

6 The man kept forgetting everything.
He was forget_____.

7 The ostrich cannot fly. It is flight_____.

8 She is always smiling. She is cheer_____.

9 The woman could not get to sleep.
She had a sleep_____ night.

10 The old man had nowhere to live.
He was home_____.

11 I help my teacher at playtime.
I am help_____.

12 The film went on and on.
It seemed end_____.

Colour
your
score

Plurals

Write the correct **plural** of each word.

1 donkey _____

2 key _____

3 party _____

4 chimney _____

5 story _____

6 monkey _____

7 jelly _____

8 nappy _____

9 cherry _____

10 trolley _____

11 city _____

12 valley _____

13 daisy _____

14 kidney _____

15 memory _____

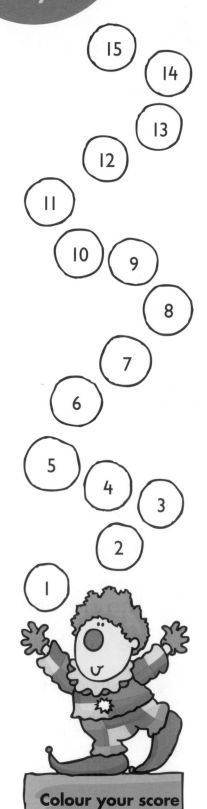

Remember y changes to ies and ey changes to eys.

15 14 13 12 11 10 9 8 7 6 5 4 3 2 1

Colour your score

22

-sure, -sion and -tion

Choose the word that fits each clue.

measure treasure pleasure division invasion

The s and t sound similar in sion and tion.

1 A chest of gold. _____

2 Another word for sharing. _____

3 Find out the size of something. _____

4 An army takes over another country. _____

5 Great enjoyment. _____

station punctuation operation fiction addition

6 The thief was taken to the police _____.

7 Story books are called _____.

8 Adding up is called _____.

9 _____ includes full stops and capital letters.

10 My gran went to hospital for an _____.

Colour your score

23

Suffixes: -ly

Complete these sentences by adding ly to the adjectives.

Adding ly to adjectives turns them into adverbs.

1 The boy ran quick____ along the road.

2 The hooter sounded loud____.

3 I tiptoed quiet____ up the stairs.

4 I proud____ went to collect my prize.

5 The cat brave____ faced up to the fierce dog.

6 The children sang beautiful____.

7 I am certain____ going to enjoy the film.

8 We shared the sweets even____.

9 I'll leave the house at exact____ half past ten.

10 The dog shook the cuddly toy rough____.

11 The girl selfish____ snatched all the cherries.

12 My mum brushed my hair careful____.

12
11
10
9
8
7
6
5
4
3
2
1

Colour your score

Rhyming words

Draw lines to join the words that rhyme.

Sometimes rhyming words have different spellings.

1. moan   white
2. light   chew
3. mane   pail
4. blue   tone
5. whale   pain

6. soap   flea
7. seen   fair
8. there   hope
9. two   mean
10. bee   shoe

11. great   coast
12. could   bun
13. most   such
14. won   late
15. hutch   wood

Colour your score

ar and or words

Write **ar** or **or** in the gap to make a real word.

1 b___k

2 c___k

3 c___n

4 b___ge

5 c___ve

6 f___k

7 h___sh

8 h___m

9 h___n

10 h___p

11 n___th

12 m___ch

13 t___ch

14 l___ge

15 s___t

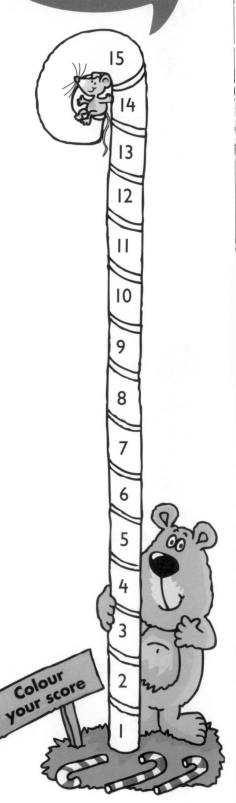

Read the words out loud to discover which is correct.

15
14
13
12
11
10
9
8
7
6
5
4
3
2
1

Colour your score

26

Words to practise

Practise these words and then write one in each sentence.

| behind   climb   most   because |
| after   water   beautiful |
| everybody   sure   break |

Remember, you will spell the words correctly if you practise.

1 The sunset was _____ to look at.

2 Are you _____ you can come to my house?

3 He didn't go to school _____ he had a cold.

4 I will _____ up the ladder and rescue the kitten.

5 _____ people like cheese.

6 The boys went swimming _____ school.

7 When the teacher asked a question _____ put up their hands.

8 The smallest kitten got left _____.

9 Be careful or you will _____ that glass.

10 I was thirsty so I had a drink of _____.

10
9
8
7
6
5
4
3
2
1

Colour your score

el, le, al and il

Choose el, le, al or il to end each word.

1. tab____

2. cam____

3. med____

4. penc____

5. tunn____

6. ped____

7. foss____

8. app____

9. squirr____

10. nostr____

11. hospit____

12. litt____

13. puzz____

14. tow____

15. anim____

Try out each spelling if you don't know it already.

15
14
13
12
11
10
9
8
7
6
5
4
3
2
1

Colour your score

Silent letters

Write **gn**, **wr** or **kn** at the beginning of each word.

Some words have letters at the beginning that you don't sound out.

1 I ___ap a scarf around my neck in winter.

2 The ___ight wore armour and carried a sword.

3 My nan loves to ___it my jumpers.

4 The dog started to ___aw on the bone.

5 I saw the ___eck of an old ship.

6 I had to ___ock on the door.

7 I wear a watch on my left ___ist.

8 The ___at bite on my leg itches.

9 I fell over and hurt my ___ee.

10 I can ___ite very neatly.

11 There is a painted ___ome in next door's garden.

12 A ___en is a small brown bird.

13 The opposite of right is ___ong.

14 I don't ___ow where I put my pencil.

Colour your score

a for o

Use each clue to write a word with an **a** sounding like **o**.

Remember, **a** doesn't always sound like **o** after **w, wh or qu.**

1 What you do to get clean.
w_____

2 You can wear this so you know the time. w_____

3 What an elephant would do if it sat on a hat. squ_____

4 This striped insect might sting you. w_____

5 Another name for an argument. qu_____

6 Another way of saying I would like. w_____

Choose a word to finish each sentence.

was	quality	what	wander

7 I always choose apples of the best _____.

8 The horse _____ brown and white.

9 I like to _____ about in the fields.

10 Will you tell me _____ you are doing?

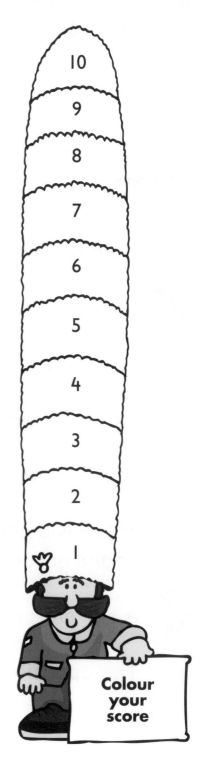

10
9
8
7
6
5
4
3
2
1

Colour your score

More words to practise

Practise spelling the words and then write the correct one in each sentence.

Remember, practice makes perfect!

should	could	class	money
great	mind	who	hour	only
people	again	many

1 I wonder _____ our new teacher will be.

2 I wish I _____ go to the fair with my friends.

3 There were crowds of _____ on the beach.

4 I have so _____ toys in my bedroom.

5 If you change your _____, you can still come.

6 I am seven but my sister is _____ two.

7 I had a _____ time at the circus.

8 There are twenty children in my _____.

9 I have a lot of _____ in my purse.

10 My dad said I _____ be able to count to 100.

11 I had to wait for one _____ at the doctor's.

12 I enjoyed the film so much I would like to see it _____.

Colour your score

12
11
10
9
8
7
6
5
4
3
2
1

Answers

er, ir and ur
1. girl
2. verb
3. curl
4. church
5. herb
6. bird
7. stir
8. burst
9. dirt
10. her
11. first
12. Thursday
13. hurt
14. term
15. person

Plurals: –s or –es
1. banana<u>s</u>
2. hedge<u>s</u>
3. book<u>s</u>
4. witch<u>es</u>
5. duck<u>s</u>
6. buz<u>zes</u>
7. kite<u>s</u>
8. match<u>es</u>
9. dish<u>es</u>
10. frog<u>s</u>
11. leg<u>s</u>
12. bus<u>es</u>
13. bank<u>s</u>
14. hutch<u>es</u>
15. cow<u>s</u>

Word endings: –tch or –ch
1. hu<u>tch</u>
2. fe<u>tch</u>
3. mu<u>ch</u>
4. ca<u>tch</u>
5. rea<u>ch</u>
6. di<u>tch</u>
7. pin<u>ch</u>
8. pa<u>tch</u>
9. ri<u>ch</u>
10. ar<u>ch</u>
11. tha<u>tch</u>
12. su<u>ch</u>
13. ma<u>tch</u>
14. bea<u>ch</u>
15. i<u>tch</u>

Wh– question words
1. What
2. Why
3. Where
4. When
5. When / What
6. Why
7. Which
8. What
9. Which
10. When
11. What
12. Which

–ing and –ed
1. farming, farmed
2. storming, stormed
3. hatching, hatched
4. kicking, kicked
5. banging, banged
6. thanking, thanked
7. hissing, hissed
8. calling, called
9. buzzing, buzzed
10. puffing, puffed
11. milking, milked
12. jumping, jumped
13. shocking, shocked
14. growling, growled
15. barking, barked

More –ing and –ed
1. humming, hummed
2. smiling, smiled
3. knitting, knitted
4. hopping, hopped
5. shaving, shaved
6. clapping, clapped
7. shading, shaded
8. skating, skated
9. chatting, chatted
10. slicing, sliced
11. skipping, skipped
12. shaping, shaped
13. robbing, robbed
14. planning, planned
15. grinning, grinned

Prefixes: un–
1. <u>un</u>block
2. <u>un</u>equal
3. <u>un</u>hook
4. <u>un</u>happy
5. <u>un</u>pack
6. <u>un</u>even
7. <u>un</u>able
8. <u>un</u>cover
9. <u>un</u>clear
10. <u>un</u>afraid
11. <u>un</u>kind
12. <u>un</u>helpful
13. <u>un</u>plug
14. <u>un</u>ripe
15. <u>un</u>well

–ve words
1. hive
2. arrive
3. brave
4. live
5. gave
6. cave
7. above
8. love
9. five
10. drive

–er and –est
1. longer, longest
2. shorter, shortest
3. taller, tallest
4. thicker, thickest
5. softer, softest
6. brighter, brightest
7. darker, darkest
8. madder, maddest
9. redder, reddest
10. larger, largest
11. simpler, simplest
12. nicer, nicest
13. thinner, thinnest
14. bigger, biggest
15. gentler, gentlest

Apostrophes
1. the dog's bone
2. the man's hat
3. the girl's hair
4. the boy's socks
5. the cat's whiskers
6. the lady's shoes
7. the car's horn
8. the elephant's trunk
9. the train's whistle
10. the pig's curly tail
11. the bird's wing
12. the cow's calf
13. the windmill's sails
14. the horse's saddle
15. the mouse's nest

Changing y to i
1. sillier, silliest
2. angrier, angriest
3. happier, happiest
4. heavier, heaviest
5. cries, cried
6. marries, married
7. hurries, hurried
8. fries, fried
9. babies
10. families
11. lorries
12. ladies

Suffixes: –ment or –ness
1. darkness
2. payment
3. illness
4. amazement
5. entertainment
6. rudeness
7. brightness
8. kindness
9. excitement
10. punishment
11. sadness
12. enjoyment

Syllables
1. 2
2. 3
3. 3
4. 3
5. 5
6. 4
7. 3
8. 2
9. 3
10. 2
11. 3
12. 3
13. 4
14. 4
15. 3